SYLVIA PLATH'S
TOMATO SOUP CAKE

A COMPENDIUM OF Classic Authors' Favourite Recipes

SYLVIA PLATH'S TOMATO SOUP CAKE

faber

First published in 2024
by Faber & Faber Ltd
The Bindery, 51 Hatton Garden
London EC1N 8HN

Typeset by Faber & Faber Ltd
Printed in the UK by CPI Group (UK) Ltd, Croydon, CR0 4YY

A CIP record for this book
is available from the British Library

ISBN 978-0-571-39036-6

2 4 6 8 10 9 7 5 3

Contents

Foreword
by Bee Wilson

Are the focused demands of the writing life compatible with the patient work of cooking? Sometimes yes and sometimes no is the answer, based on the volume you hold in your hand.

Some of the writers collected here freely admit to being 'bad cookers', as Beryl Bainbridge puts it, quoting her children. Bainbridge's 'Instant Mince' is one of the most bracingly no-frills recipes I've ever read, consisting of mince boiled 'furiously' for no more than fifteen minutes with '3 lb of potatoes, two sliced onions, a tin of tomatoes and a teaspoon of vinegar'. Bainbridge does not indicate how the potatoes should be prepared. The whole mélange is designed to be served over fluffy white bread with raw onions, HP sauce and a cup of strong tea.

Time in the kitchen is time away from the typewriter or the pen and paper so it's no wonder that many writers have seen cooking as a drag.

Perhaps the most adamant non-cook in the volume is Dodie Smith, of *The Hundred and One Dalmatians* fame. 'When I was poor,' Smith writes, 'I got my food at cheap restaurants. When I made money I got someone to cook for me.' Smith's recipe for 'Proper Strawberry Shortcake' actually sounds delicious, even though the ratio of butter to flour is on the low side. Smith explains that she has never actually made it, 'of course'.

Then there are the writers who give the air of having cooked something but whose instructions are so wildly off as to sow seeds of doubt. Jack Kerouac springs to mind. His 'Green Pea Soup' – which he describes as 'excellent' – consists of dried Lipton pea-soup mix (which would have come in powdered form) simmered with fried bacon and onions for a grand total of 'a minute'. Given that Kerouac never asks us to add any water to the soup the question of how it can be simmered is a mystery. If you followed his recipe, you would end up with a weird salty sludge with chunks of uncooked onions. Excellent, Jack? Really?

Yet just when you are starting to wonder whether all writers – literary ones, anyway – have a vendetta against cooking, you come across Christopher Isherwood's recipe for chocolate brownies, which is so meticulous that it could have been triple-tested in the Ottolenghi Test Kitchen. Isherwood asks us not only to sift the flour and the baking powder but to 're-sift' the flour twice over. He reminds us three times of the importance of blending everything 'thoroughly and energetically'. Isherwood apparently belongs to the same school of cookery as Truman Capote, whose 'Cold Banana Pudding' recipe comprises fourteen very precise steps ('beat 3 reserved egg whites until foamy').

Some writers channel the intelligence of their writing into the act of cooking. Consider Vladimir Nabokov's recipe for boiled eggs. I doubt anyone will ever write a better egg recipe. It is the ideal combination of precise timings (the eggs are cooked for somewhere between 200 and 240 seconds) and sensory cues. 'Let them slip soundlessly into the (boiling) water,' Nabokov tells us: a perfect description of how to add eggs to water. He even helpfully explains that 'bubbles mean it is boiling' rather than assuming that we just *know*.

I wish I had had Nabokov's egg recipe in my twenties, when I wasted so much time experimenting with different methods for boiling eggs. Every (egg-eating) young person should be given a copy of this book when they leave school so that they can make Nabokov's boiled eggs for themselves and their friends.

Read Nabokov's recipe side by side with Bainbridge's. Both are arrestingly memorable pieces of writing and they offer opposing visions of how cooking and writing might coexist in a writer's life. On the one hand, we have a writer (Bainbridge) who has given so much to her art that there is almost nothing left for cooking. On the other, there is Nabokov, who brings the same luminous precision to his eggs that he brings to his prose. He writes of the egg that cracks in the water 'and starts to disgorge a cloud of white stuff like a medium in an old-fashioned seance'.

Nabokov is not alone in relishing the way food looks and tastes as it cooks. This book is teeming with delicious images and similes, such as Margery Allingham beating her salad cream until 'thick as honey'. I love being told by Laurie

Colwin (very much a writer-cook) that she likes her zucchini fritters 'the size of a demitasse saucer'. And Allen Ginsberg's thought that after you add lemon and sugar to borscht, the red liquid becomes 'sweet & sour like lemonade'.

Recipes are like magic potions. They promise transformations. In the hands of a writer, those transformations can take unexpected directions. At the end of Katherine Mansfield's mysterious and tempting recipe for orange soufflé there is a sudden plot twist. The soufflé mix is poured into a dish with cake at the bottom 'sopped in sherry wine' with jam, and it suddenly becomes something Mansfield calls a 'party pudding'.

The best writing is always a kind of truth-telling. Some of my favourite moments in this collection are the ones where I feel a writer is both acknowledging and rebelling against the constraints of the recipe form. Ursula K. Le Guin, for example, in her recipe for 'Crab Nebula', tells us to 'add about ½ pound? 2 cups? – Well, add enough crab'. 'Add enough' is good allpurpose cooking advice. And Angela Carter says in her recipe for potato soup that there 'isn't any point' in her telling us precise amounts of leek and potato because it depends 'on the amount of soup you want to make, and what you can afford'.

Recipes in cookbooks sometimes exude a false idea of finality: that this is the only way to do something. But the enterprise of real cooking (as with writing) is full of afterthoughts and revisions. Norman Mailer's recipe for stuffed mushrooms ends with him confessing that he has 'omitted one vital detail', which is that the mushrooms must be brushed with butter and baked before they are stuffed and baked again. It's a brilliant rhetorical device which gives a simple mushroom recipe a feeling of suspense.

In the end, what the non-cooking and cooking writers in this collection have in common – and the reason this volume is such a joy – is that their recipes all contain atmospheric details that make you see and taste and smell the food on the page. I haven't yet cooked Agatha Christie's salad of green beans with its indulgent mixture of fried bacon and potted shrimps, plus vinegar, but thinking about it makes me hungry.

As Georges Simenon observes in his recipe for veal with sorrel forcemeat, the pleasure of eating sometimes feels very like 'sniffing an atmosphere'. This whole book is full of atmospheres you can sniff.

I.

STARTERS

Angela Carter's
Potato Soup

Some years ago, long enough for the conversation I am about to describe to have taken place with straight faces, in all seriousness, a friend said to me: 'I'm seriously worried about the place of the intellectual after the Revolution.' I misunderstood her completely: I said: 'As for me, I shall cook.' I assumed, you understand, that she was wondering what she, as an intellectual (which she was and is), would do with her time in a society where the profession of intellectual as such had been rendered redundant and we weren't allowed to be parasites on the backs of those in productive labour any more. And I thought, a job in the communal kitchens . . . turning out bowls, plates and dishes of hearty fare – potato soup, beans with sausage, braised oxtail, cabbage pancakes, chilli . . . all the things I knew best how to cook, due to a life spent on a relatively limited income in mostly northern climates (except for four months in Texas, where the chilli originated).

I visualised the communal kitchens as serving establishments rather like the war-time British restaurants I remember from my early childhood, where you could get a square meal for a few pennies if you'd been bombed out, or worked late at the factory, or couldn't find anything to cook in the shops. I still think that no neighbourhood should be without an eating place like that, and I still cook, basically, in the style of the Utopian cafeteria and, since it turned out that neither of us need have seriously worried about our roles once the struggle was over, I still make my living by writing. I am a middle-aged non-vegetarian yet nevertheless of the whole-food tendency, whose small son has never tasted Coca-Cola.

A small amount of chopped onion; a slightly larger amount of leeks; a much larger amount of potatoes; enough chicken or vegetable stock; milk.

This is a basic vegetable soup that could be made with leftover mashed potatoes in a pinch.

There isn't any point in giving precise amounts of ingredients for this; it depends on the amount of soup you want to make, and what you can afford. Potatoes are cheaper than leeks so, if poor, use more potatoes. Start by melting a spoonful of chopped onion in butter in a big saucepan. Then add shredded leeks – use the outer skins and the tops, the bits and pieces that are left after cooking the white, tender insides in a cheese sauce or making a salad of them with a French dressing. (You have to boil your leeks until they are tender before you can do either of these things with them, by the way, but this is not a recipe for leek cheese or leek salad, so I will give no further details. This is a recipe for potato soup.) Sweat the shredded leeks in the melted butter for a while. The more leeks you use, the more leek flavour the soup will have. Then add the peeled and chopped potatoes. The more potatoes you add, the more body the soup will have. The potato flavour will depend on the variety of potatoes you use. Try the variety called Désirée. Why not. What a terrific name for a potato. Don't even think of wasting those expensive Cypriot potatoes in a soup like this. They will not dissolve. Chop your potatoes up finely, or grate them. If you use leftover mashed potatoes, do not add them until the leeks are so limp they are almost cooked. Otherwise, add the potatoes to the leeks and let them sweat together. When they have sweated sufficiently, cover the vegetables up with stock and let them swim a while. Simmer until everything is soft. Sieve. Add milk until the soup reaches the consistency you prefer. Reheat. Salt it and pepper it. Add dill seeds if you like the aniseed flavour. A spoonful of cream or sour cream stirred in before serving is a refinement. You can always leave the leeks out if they are too expensive. Then you really do need dill or sour cream – or yoghurt will do – and a bit more onion, to start with, or it can get to be like liquidised mashed potatoes. Do not even think of using margarine instead of butter in this recipe. At this level of subsistence food, you need all the calories you can get.

Laurie Colwin's
Zucchini Fritters

Most people think fried food is fun and not serious eating. A crisp little fritter slips right down (often as a mere vehicle for the catsup or tomato sauce), but never mind that it is fried: it is all for a good cause.

Zucchini make wonderful fritter material, especially small, young ones roughly the size of a lead pencil. If necessary you can use those enormous overgrown zucchini that gardeners are always palming off on their friends in the fall.

Shred the zucchini – use four small ones – and drain on a towel. Separate two eggs and beat the whites until fairly stiff. Add half a cup of milk to the egg yolk, beat and add about half to three-quarters of a cup of flour – the batter should be a little thicker than pancake batter. Add the zucchini, salt, pepper and some chopped scallion. Fold in the egg whites and fry in clarified butter (or unclarified butter) or olive oil until golden on both sides. Some people like large fritters. I like mine the size of a demitasse saucer. Of course these are not fritters in the strict sense of the term. Rather they are pancakes. As to their being fried, my motto about fried vegetables is: 'Fried eggplant today, ratatouille tomorrow!'

Ian Fleming's Scrambled Eggs

For four individualists:

  12 fresh eggs
  Salt and pepper
  5–6 oz of fresh butter

Break the eggs into a bowl. Beat thoroughly with a fork and season well. In a small copper (or heavy-bottomed) saucepan melt 4 oz of the butter. When melted, pour in the eggs and cook over a very low heat, whisking continuously with a small egg whisk.

While the eggs are slightly more moist than you would wish for eating, remove pan from heat, add rest of butter and continue whisking for half a minute, adding the while finely chopped chives or fine herbs. Serve on hot buttered toast in individual copper dishes (for appearance only) with pink champagne (Taittinger) and low music.

Allen Ginsberg's Cold Summer Borscht

Dozen beets cleaned & chopped to bite-size salad-size strips. Stems & leaves also chopped like salad lettuce. All boiled together lightly salted to make a bright red soup, with beets now soft – boil an hour or more. Add sugar & lemon juice to make the red liquid sweet & sour like lemonade.

Chill 4 gallon(s) of beet liquid – serve with:
1) Sour cream on table
2) Boiled small or halved potato on the side i.e. so hot potatoes don't heat the cold soup prematurely
3) Spring salad on table to put into cold red liquid

     1) Onions – sliced (spring onions)

     2) Tomatoes – sliced bite-sized

     3) Lettuce – ditto

     4) Cucumbers – ditto

     5) A few radishes

Robert Graves's
Mock Anchovy Pâté

This recipe is taken from Apicius's cookery book, Artis magiricae *(first century AD).*

Take fillets of grilled or boiled fish (preferably white fish) and mince enough of these to fill a pan of the size required. Add a few peppercorns pounded with rue, moisten with vegetable stock, break in an egg or two, pour in a little olive oil, and mix up everything in the pan until it forms a smooth, solid mixture. On top of this place a covering of small jellyfish, taking care that they do not mix with the eggs. Then cook in steam (to prevent their mixing with the eggs) and when they have dried out, sprinkle with pepper and serve. Nobody at the table will know what he is eating.

Jack Kerouac's
Green Pea Soup

Package Lipton Green Pea Soup
Bacon
Onions
Salt & pepper

Simply fry chopped bacon till the pieces are crisped dark brown, then throw the onions and spiced soup mix into bacon and sizzling fat, and stir. Let simmer for a minute for excellent pea soup.

Norman Mailer's Stuffed Mushrooms

I've given this recipe once or twice before. Since it's adapted almost directly from a recipe in Larousse, I can't lay claim to huge originality. In any event, it's Stuffed Mushrooms.

You chop the stems, squeeze as much water out of them as you can, which is the trickiest part of the whole dish; you have to use dish towels and do it again and again. Then sauté the chopped mushroom with onions very finely chopped, shallots (if you have them) and a good amount of garlic. I give no proportions in this, because it's the sort of dish that must be cooked to the temperament of the chef. The sautéeing, incidentally, must be done with a lavish use of quarter-pound sticks of sweet butter.

When it's all going nicely, grate in fresh nutmeg, quite a bit, and a good amount of black pepper. Then set aside to cool. Indeed, you can do better than that and set it in the refrigerator. This is not only for ease in handling but, I swear, improves the flavour.

Then take the caps, fill them with cold stuffing (which is now called *duxelles*) and sprinkle them with a mix of bread crumbs, a bit of cinnamon, salt, pepper, mustard powder and grated lemon peel, all of which makes a heavy dust on top of the stuffed mushrooms. Then put it in and bake for five minutes.

I've omitted one vital detail. Before the caps are stuffed, brush the top sides with butter and bake them on a flat dish for five minutes. Then remove, stuff, and lay on a buttered slab or tinfoil; put it back in the oven for five minutes. Remove. That's it.

Vladimir Nabokov's
Eggs à la Nabocoque

Boil water in a saucepan (bubbles mean it is boiling!). Take two eggs (for one person) out of the refrigerator. Hold them under the hot tap water to make them ready for what awaits them.

Place each in a pan, one after the other, and let them slip soundlessly into the (boiling) water. Consult your wristwatch. Stand over them with a spoon preventing them (they are apt to roll) from knocking against the damned side of the pan. If, however, an egg cracks in the water (now bubbling like mad) and starts to disgorge a cloud of white stuff like a medium in an old-fashioned seance, fish it out and throw it away. Take another and be more careful. After 200 seconds have passed, or, say, 240 (taking interruptions into account), start scooping the eggs out. Place them, round end up, in two egg cups. With a small spoon tap-tap in a circle and then pry open the lid of the shell. Have some salt and buttered bread (white) ready. Eat.

V. N. November 18, 1972.

Stephen Spender's
Pâté Maison

8 oz chicken livers

4 oz butter

2 oz cream

1 oz brandy

Good pinch ground cloves

Pinch mace

Pinch nutmeg

Pinch thyme

Black pepper

Salt

½ pint (US 1 ¼ cups) aspic jelly

Parsley

Sauté the chicken livers in 1 oz butter. Put in a liquidiser with the remaining butter, cream, brandy, cloves, mace, nutmeg, thyme, and seasoning, and blend. Leave to cool. Coat a mould with aspic jelly and put in the refrigerator to set. When set put pâté into the mould and return to the refrigerator to harden. Then turn out and decorate with parsley. Serve with black olives, radishes and hot toast. (Serves 4.)

MAINS

Beryl Bainbridge's
Instant Mince

I am a very bad cooker, as the children put it. It could stem from my father's habit of doing all the cooking at home – he wore his ARP uniform and made things like rubber egg and boiled tomatoes. However, I do have one recipe truly my own.

Take ½ lb of mince, 3 lb of potatoes, two sliced onions, a tin of tomatoes and a teaspoon of vinegar.

Throw the whole lot into a pan, though not the tin holding the tomatoes, and boil furiously for less than 15 minutes. Let the pan almost boil dry.

Cut one huge slice of fluffy white bread and spread thickly with butter. Spoon the instant mince on to the bread and cover with HP sauce, also raw onion rings.

Eat with a very strong cup of tea.

Agatha Christie's Hot Bean Salad

Take a sufficient quantity of *freshly cooked hot French beans* for 6 people. Put in a brown casserole and mix with *freshly milled pepper* and *2–3 tablespoons of vinegar*. Add ½ lb *chopped-up bacon, fried*, to which has been added in the frying pan a *carton of potted shrimps*. Mix all together and serve with the *hot fat* from frying pan poured over it.

N.B. Runner beans can be used if preferred.

Joan Didion's Mexican Chicken

Chicken breasts: 1 whole breast per person
Onions: ½ per person
Tomatoes: ½ per person
Fresh chiles: see below
Garlic: 1 clove per person
Salt & pepper

This is very simple and takes about half an hour if you have cooked the chicken breasts ahead. If you haven't, poach them in water with an onion, a carrot, celery tops, bay leaf, whatever: remove the chicken from the bones (usually I throw the bones back into the pot to make stock, but the stock has nothing to do with the recipe) and tear into rather large bite-sized pieces. Set the chicken aside.

Slice the onions and sauté until limp in a little olive oil. Add the chopped garlic (if you're doing this in quantity you cut down the amount of garlic) and the chopped fresh chiles. The amount of chile depends on the heat of the particular chile available; I use very hot small serrano green chiles and chop maybe three for six people. Chop the tomatoes roughly and add to the onion mixture. (The amount of tomato you use should also decrease if you make a large amount, or the sauce will be watery.) Add salt and pepper; cook five or ten minutes, uncovered, over low heat; add the chicken, mix thoroughly and cook only until heated through. This can be kept warm for quite a while but if you keep cooking it, the tomato turns watery and the chicken gets stringy.

Serve with hot tortillas, a bowl of guacamole, a bowl of fresh cilantro, a bowl of sour cream and a fresh salsa. (The salsa is made by chopping up more chiles and mixing with a little chopped onion, a little tomato, some cilantro leaves and a splash of cold water.) The idea is to break off bits of tortilla and wrap it around bits of chicken and anything else you want and eat it with your fingers. I do this all the time as a main course, usually with a chilled cucumber or watercress soup first and a banana tart or flan for dessert.

Stella Gibbons's Savoury Rice

'It is Extremely Filling,' says Miss Gibbons. *'It's cheap, and men love it.'*

Method: Fry a clove of garlic in margarine until it is brown. Then put into the pan a breakfast-cupful of cooked rice that has been washed before cooking (more rice can be used if you want more, of course) and keep on stirring it until it has absorbed the fat. Then put in curry powder to taste, the pulp and seeds of three tomatoes, and a third of a cupful of currants and sultanas (well washed, of course). A dash of salt, pepper and lemon juice improves it. (You need to be careful and choice with the seasoning, or there is a risk of the dish becoming merely rich and sticky.)

If the average housewife is scared of garlic, she can use onion.

The dish goes well with a plain salad of lettuce leaves dressed sharply with vinegar and salt (but you might as well say a plain salad of gold leaf, with the prices lettuces can be during wartime).

Aldous Huxley's
Gnocchi di Patate

Boil 2 lb of potatoes. Peel and put through a sieve while still hot. Mix with ½ lb of flour. Add salt to taste. Work thoroughly together. Roll the mixture into finger-thick strips and cut these strips into 1 ½ inch sections. Meanwhile boil 2 quarts of salted water. While the water is boiling, throw half the gnocchi into the saucepan. As they come to the surface, scoop them out and add others. Pour a little melted butter over the gnocchi and sprinkle with grated cheese. Gravy or tomato sauce may be used instead of the butter.

Ursula K. Le Guin's
Crab Nebula

Make a cream sauce with tablespoon butter, 2 tablespoons flour, 1 cup milk. Add about one cup grated Tillamook cheese (or more – or less . . . if you are unable to obtain Tillamook you may use any inferior American Cheddar, but the difference will be noticeable, unless you have a calloused palate).

Now add about ½ pound? 2 cups? – Well, add enough crab. (If you are unable to obtain Pacific crab, you may use those flabby little Atlantic ones, or even lobster; but if you are reduced to king crab, forget it.)

Flavour with sherry to taste, salt, pepper, parsley.

Serve on rice, or wild rice if you are J. Paul Getty, or English muffins, or whatever.

Rosamond Lehmann's
Anna Woodhouse's Pie

This is an extravagant way of doing what is normally a fairly economical meal, but I feel it justifies the extra money spent because it transforms Shepherd's Pie into a really sublime dinner-party meal.

Large onion, chopped, 2–3 cloves garlic, chopped, 3 tablespoons oil, 1 lb good minced beef or lamb, small tin tomatoes or ½ lb chopped tomatoes or 1 tablespoon tomato concentrate, ½ pint red or dry white wine, ½ pint appropriate stock, 3 heaped teaspoons cornflour, salt, pepper, parsley, grated rind of half an orange, ½ teaspoon of cinnamon.

Soften the onion and garlic slowly in the oil. Raise heat, add the mince and brown. Mix in tomatoes or concentrate, wine and half the stock. Simmer for 10–15 minutes until the meat is tender. Slake cornflour with half the remaining stock, add to the meat with all the seasonings, parsley and spices. Simmer for 5 minutes. Add remaining stock only if mixture seems dry.

Put mixture in heat-proof dish, top with mashed potato, sprinkle with 2 tablespoons grated Cheddar. Bake 10 minutes at Regulo 6 (400°), and then 45 minutes at Regulo 4 (350°).

Doris Lessing's
Chicken with Lemon and Orange

1 chicken
Garlic
Pepper
Salt
Rind and juice 2 oranges
Rind and juice 1–2 lemons
Butter

Rub the chicken with garlic, pepper and salt to taste. Fill the cavity with the orange and lemon juice and strips of orange and lemon rind. Roast with butter in a moderate oven (375 degrees F or Gas Mark 4). Baste during cooking at least 3 times with the juices from the cavity. At the end of the cooking turn heat up so that the bird is well browned. The juices should caramelise a little. Cut the chicken into pieces. Serve with green salad. (Serves 4.)

Olivia Manning's Barbecue Lamb

This recipe calls for a number of ingredients and a little trouble but should turn a leg of frozen lamb into a dish as tender and as rich in flavour as Pekin Duck.

Rub powdered mustard, powdered ginger, salt and freshly ground pepper into a leg of lamb. Split the garlic and stick into cuts in lean part of meat. Dredge meat with flour and roast in a hot oven Regulo 6 or 7 (450°) for 30 minutes.

Prepare a basting sauce of 2 tablespoons sugar, 1 tablespoon vinegar, a dash each of Worcester sauce, mushroom ketchup, brown sauce and cayenne, and add a sliced onion, 2 cloves of garlic crushed with salt, and 1 oz melted butter.

When the lamb has roasted for 30 minutes, pour on sauce and start basting. Cook until meat is tender and of a 'crumbling' consistency. Watch that liquid does not dry, and add water or vegetable stock as required. Gravy should be rich and brown. It may be strained over meat, but if served separately, extra liquid may be added.

Ngaio Marsh's
Steak en Casserole

4 oz butter

½ pint wine

1 clove garlic, crushed

Bay leaves

Bouquet garni

Salt

Black pepper

4–6 oz steak per person

Egg, beaten

Coarse oatmeal

Mushrooms

Tomatoes

Make a marinade of the butter melted in the wine. Add the garlic, bay leaves, bouquet garni, salt and black pepper. Put the steak in the marinade. Allow the steak to remain in it for approximately 24 hours. Then remove the steak and dip in the egg. Coat with the oatmeal. Place in a casserole with enough of the marinade to cover. Cook at a very low temperature in the oven (275°F or Gas Mark 1) for 4–6 hours until the steak absorbs the marinade and comes to seething point. Serve with mushrooms and peeled tomatoes, cooked in the liquor.

Georges Simenon's
Fricandeau à l'Oseille

2 lb fillet of veal

Very fine lardons pork

1–2 carrots, diced

1–2 onions, diced

Bouquet garni of parsley, bay leaves and thyme

1 or 2 cloves

¼ pint stock

Salt and pepper

For the sorrel forcemeat:

4–5 handfuls sorrel

½ oz butter

Lard the surface of the veal with the very fine lardons of pork. Place the meat in a stewing dish, add the diced carrots, onions, bouquet garni, cloves and the stock. Season with salt and pepper. Cover and cook in a slow oven (300°F or

Gas Mark 2). Baste often while cooking so that the meat takes a lovely golden colour.

After 2 ½ hours the meat will be cooked. The gravy must then be transferred to a small saucepan and reduced slowly.

To make the sorrel forcemeat take the sorrel, pare, cut away stalks and wash well. Then place the sorrel in a saucepan or casserole on a low heat to reduce. When it is half reduced, add the butter, cooking until sorrel is puréed. Pour the veal gravy over the sorrel.

To serve set the meat on a bed of the sorrel forcemeat. (Serves 4.)

Note.

Which dish do I like best? It is sometimes difficult for me to make a distinction between taste and smell, between the pleasure of eating and the pleasure of sniffing an atmosphere.

When away from America, for example, I dream about the thick smell of eggs and bacon, with the more subtle coffee fragrance coming out of all quiet little places along the roads, even though my favourite American dish is clam chowder.

In London, haddock is my first choice for breakfast, in Holland, soft white bread with creamy cheese.

What about Paris? For me, as for my friend Maigret, the most genuine smell of the little bistros as well as that of the *loges de concierges*, the smell of old, narrow streets and of creaking staircases, is given by *le fricandeau à l'oseille*. Alas! It's not always easy to find fresh sorrel in America (I used to plant some in my garden, in Connecticut) but, if you are a lucky one, you can try the above recipe and, for a few hours, your home will have the aroma of a centuries-old house in Paris.

Noel Streatfeild's
Filets de Bœuf aux Bananas

I have to admit that I am normally a very bad cook. However, I met this dish at a house I was staying in and liked it so much that I wrote it down and practised it at home.

2 lb fillet beef, 2 bananas, 1 small onion, ½ gill cream, 1 egg yolk and a little of each: flour, butter, lard, breadcrumbs, horseradish sauce and chopped parsley.

Remove fat from the meat, cut fillets one inch thick and shape and trim neatly. Beat them out flatter, then fry in a mixture of butter and lard for 8 minutes (make sure fat is very hot before adding the fillets). Press fillets down as they cook and keep turning them. Put to one side in a warm dish.

Peel the bananas and cut into longish pieces but not too thick. Coat the pieces in flour then egg and breadcrumbs and fry. Add prepared bananas to the dish of fillets.

Make an egg sauce by chopping the onion finely and cooking in water for a few minutes. Strain off water and sauté the onion in a little butter. Add the egg yolk and cream. Stir over a gentle heat until it thickens, but be careful not to boil it. Add a little horseradish sauce. Pour this sauce over the fillets and bananas and sprinkle the whole dish with parsley.

Sylvia Townsend Warner's Chintz Turbot

Fillet a small turbot (halibut will do). Simmer the bones. Cook the fillets slowly in butter and a little milk then put to one side in a warmed dish. Make a bechamel sauce using the fish stock; flavour with a little tarragon vinegar. Add to this sauce a good handful of shelled shrimps and, if you can get it, a spot or two of spinach essence to colour the sauce lightly green. Cover the turbot fillets with the sauce and sprinkle with tarragon.

I serve this with an endive salad with a special dressing of two-thirds cream, one-third sherry, freshly ground pepper and salt.

Margery Allingham's
Salad Cream

1 tablespoon sugar

1 tablespoon salt

2 tablespoons mustard

1 teaspoon celery salt

1 teacup salad oil

4 eggs

2 teacups vinegar

1 teacup milk

1 teacup creamy milk

Mix the sugar, salts and mustard together in a large basin then add gradually the salad oil. Beat the eggs and add to the mixture then add the vinegar and milk. Stand the basin in boiling water and stir till thick as honey. When cold add the creamy milk. Bottle and cover. This salad cream will keep for one year.

Barbara Pym's Marmalade

3 large Seville oranges

1 lemon

3 pints water (plus pips' water)

1 kilo (2.2 lbs) plus half a pound sugar

Boiling time for set 30 minutes. Made about 5 lbs.

Rebecca West's
Dutch Onion Crisps

12 small onions

2 cupfuls cooked peas (approximately 1 lb
   after shelling)

3 oz butter or margarine

2 tablespoonsful flour

1 teacupful minced walnut kernels

1 teacupful breadcrumbs

½ pint milk

½ pint water

Method: Peel the onions and boil them in the milk together with the water, and when tender remove the onions from the saucepan, taking care not to break them. Now grease a baking tin (about 10 inches by 8 inches) and place in it the onions, covering them with peas. Make a sauce by melting the butter in a stewpan, working in the flour, then the milk and water the onions were boiled in, and seasoning to taste. Pour over onions and peas. Now mix the walnuts and breadcrumbs together and bind with enough oiled butter or margarine to make a stiff mixture and spread over. Bake in a hot oven until a golden brown – about 20 minutes.

Tennessee Williams's Grits

I'm afraid I have no rare recipes to offer as I seldom cook. When I do, I nearly always prepare a rather fancy kind of grits, since like most Southerners I grew up on them. Many of my friends in Key West are from the North and are not at all adapted to them.

I use quick grits. If there's a secret to their cooking it's continual stirring and taking them off the burner at just the right thickness. I stir in 'Bacos' or bits of real bacon, cheddar cheese and oleo-margarine. I use substitute salt, so I salt mine separately.

Yankee dinner guests remain recalcitrant, but now and then a Southerner comes along who enjoys them as much as I.

DESSERTS

Kingsley Amis's
Fromage à la Crème

5 egg whites

1 lb fresh thick cream cheese

2 oz castor sugar

½ pint thick cream

Whip the egg whites to meringue stiffness. Beat the cream cheese and sugar together with a fork until absolutely smooth. Fold the whites into the cheese. Put the mixture into a muslin bag and drain for 2–3 hours in a cool place. Before serving whip the cream until stiff but still pourable. Turn cheese out on to a dish and cover with the cream. Serve cold but not from the refrigerator.

This is splendid on its own but fantastic with fresh strawberries or, better still, raspberries. (Serves 4.)

Enid Blyton's Cherry Cake

This is a cake my own children love and it is easy to make when children come to tea.

½ lb margarine
3 eggs
6 oz cherries
Few drops of vanilla essence
6 oz flour
6 oz castor sugar

Method – beat the margarine and sugar till soft and creamy, drop in eggs one by one and beat well in between each. Add flour gradually, and lastly cherries and flavouring. If too stiff, add a little milk. Bake in a moderate oven to start, then drop to Regulo 3. It takes about 1 ½ to 2 hours to bake.

This is just as nice with fruit instead of cherries, or ginger cut up is excellent.

Half the quantity makes a nice little cake for tea, but only takes ¾ to 1 hour to cook.

Brigid Brophy's
Baroque Cake

This cake looks like a lovely seventeenth-century architecture. It was devised by my daughter Kate and her boyfriend. Preparation time: 1 hour / Baking time: 50 minutes – 1 ¼ hours.

1 cup butter

1 cup sugar

5 eggs

½ cup self-rising flour, sifted

6 tablespoons strong coffee

1 ½ cups confectioners' sugar

½ cup whole coffee beans (optional)

1. To prepare cake, cream ½ cup butter and ½ cup sugar together until soft and pale.
2. Beat 2 eggs well and gradually add them to the butter mixture.
3. Add the ½ cup of flour and mix thoroughly.

4. Add ⅔ tablespoon strong coffee to taste.
5. Pour the mixture into 2 greased round 7-inch cake tins.
6. Bake at 350° for about 20 minutes or until firm to touch. Remove from the oven and allow to cool while you prepare the rest of the cake.
7. To prepare meringues beat 3 egg whites with an electric beater until they are very stiff – you should be able to turn the bowl upside down without the egg falling out.
8. Add about ½ cup regular and about ½ cup confectioners' sugar to the egg whites. Fold in well.
9. Add 3 tablespoons coffee and beat well.
10. Put dessert spoonfuls of the mixture onto a greased baking sheet. Since the meringues will spread when cooked, do not put them too close together. Make them as round as possible. (You will have about 20 small meringues.)
11. Cook for about 30 minutes to 1 hour at 250° or until crisp all the way through. Be careful to avoid burning them.

12. For butter icing, cream ½ cup butter until very soft. Add 1 cup confectioners' sugar and strong coffee to taste. Mix well.

13. To complete baroque cake, use the butter icing to sandwich the cake together. Then put a thin layer of icing on the top and sides of the cake.

14. Arrange the meringues on the cake. Push more icing between the meringues to keep them in place. You can decorate the cake with whole coffee beans.

15. Refrigerate for 15 to 30 minutes before serving. Yield: 6–8 servings.

Truman Capote's
Cold Banana Pudding

Ingredients:

- 3 ¾ cups milk
- 6 ½ oz vanilla pudding and pie mix
- 3 eggs, separated
- 1 cup heavy cream, stiffly beaten
- 2 teaspoons vanilla extract
- 12 ladyfingers
- 4 bananas, sliced thinly crosswise
- ⅛ teaspoon nutmeg
- ⅓ cup superfine sugar

Instructions:

1. In a medium saucepan, gradually blend 3 ¾ cups milk with the vanilla pudding and pie mix (NOT instant).
2. Separate 3 eggs, adding yolks to pudding mixture and reserving whites for later use.
3. Beat pudding mixture with electric or rotary beater until smooth.

4. Cook, stirring constantly, until pudding comes to a full boil.
5. Remove from heat.
6. Cover surface with foil or plastic wrap and cool for 20 to 30 minutes.
7. Then fold in 1 cup heavy cream, stiffly beaten, and 2 teaspoons vanilla extract.
8. Arrange 6 ladyfingers in bottom of a 2 ½ quart casserole or baking dish.
9. Spoon half the prepared pudding over ladyfingers and arrange 2 bananas, sliced, over top.
10. Repeat layers, sprinkling ⅛ teaspoon nutmeg on top of final banana layer.
11. Beat 3 reserved egg whites until foamy.
12. Gradually add ⅓ cup superfine sugar, beating very well until meringue is stiff.
13. Spoon over pudding.
14. Bake 7 to 8 minutes at 350 F, or until meringue is lightly browned.

T. S. Eliot's
Mrs Runcie's Pudding

This recipe is taken from a book called *Wishful Cooking* but, as a friend of the author's, I have partaken of Mrs Runcie's pudding many times. I understand that Mrs Runcie of Prestwick kept a kind of select boarding house for gentlemen who came to Prestwick to play golf, and this pudding appears to have been very popular with the gentlemen for whom she catered.

1 teacup milk

1 tablespoon sherry

½ lb strawberry jam

¼ lb castor sugar

1 teacup breadcrumbs

2 eggs

1 tablespoon brown sugar

Boil milk and breadcrumbs till firm; lay aside till cool. Beat the yolks of eggs with brown sugar and sherry. Mix with the bread and milk. Put in a pudding dish and bake till a skin forms. Take out of the oven and cover top with jam. Put back into oven and bake for another ¼ hour. Beat the whites of the eggs very stiff with castor sugar and lay on the top of the pudding. Brown slightly and serve. Serves 4.

Nora Ephron's
Bread Pudding

I said, 'Let's go to Chez Helene for the bread pudding,' and we did, and we each had two. The owner of Chez Helene gave us the bread pudding recipe when we left, and I'm going to throw it in because it's the best bread pudding I've ever eaten. It tastes like caramelised mush. Cream 2 cups sugar with 2 sticks butter. Then add 2 ½ cups milk, one 13-ounce can evaporated milk, 2 tablespoons nutmeg, 2 tablespoons vanilla, a loaf of wet bread in chunks and pieces (any bread will do, the worse the better) and 1 cup raisins. Stir to mix. Pour into a deep greased casserole and bake at 350 degrees for 2 hours, stirring after the first hour. Serve warm with hard sauce.

Elizabeth Jane Howard and Fay Maschler's Devils on Horseback

Unexpected courses provide a luxury of their own. After a light meal, a savoury is a great treat and a reason to keep going with the wine and wit.

On the Russian doll principle of cooking, this version of Devils on Horseback is fun. For 4 people, take 8 large prunes and pour boiling water over them. Leave for half an hour and then simmer them in this liquid until tender. When cool, carefully stone the prunes and stuff them with the sort of olive that, in its turn, has been stoned and filled with pimento.

Take a half-rasher of thinly sliced bacon for each prune. Stretch and flatten it and wrap around the prune. Set on a baking tin and bake in a hot oven until the bacon is crisply cooked – about 10 minutes. Let each Devil on Horseback ride on a piece of thin, hot buttered toast.

Christopher Isherwood's Brownies, Wendy

2 ½ oz bitter cooking chocolate

6 oz butter

3 eggs

8 oz castor sugar

1 ⅓ oz flour

½ teaspoon baking powder

¾ teaspoon salt

1 ½ teaspoons vanilla essence

4–5 oz pecan nuts, chopped

Melted butter

Extra flour

Melt the chocolate and the butter, blending them thoroughly. Then let cool. Beat the eggs with the sugar until the mixture is light, like mayonnaise. Add the chocolate to this. *It is important to keep blending everything thoroughly throughout this recipe.*

Sift the flour. Add the baking powder and the salt. Re-sift the mixture twice, adding more flour if necessary to make 1 ⅓ oz when the process is completed. Sift this flour mixture very gradually into the chocolate mixture, a little at a time.

After each sifting, blend thoroughly. Add the vanilla essence. Blend. Add the pecan nuts. Blend. Smear a square metal pan with butter and sprinkle with flour. Pour the chocolate mixture into the pan. Bake in a pre-heated oven (at 350 degrees F or Gas Mark 3) for 35 minutes. Let the brownie cool for 10 minutes before cutting it up.

Nothing can go wrong with this recipe, provided all the ingredients are thoroughly and energetically blended. If you want to test your will power, try making it without licking your fingers!

The recipe is, I understand, named for the daughter of the authoress of *The Perfect Hostess Cook Book* by Mildred O. Knopf, and has nothing to do with Barrie's play. If Peter Pan had eaten many of them he would never have been able to get himself airborne. They are definitely not dietetic.

Katherine Mansfield's
Orange Soufflé

Grate the rind of one orange & one lemon, put into saucepan with the juice of each, the yolks of three eggs & half a breakfast cup of sugar, stir this until it becomes the thickness of honey, beat up the whites of eggs to a <u>stiff</u> froth, & add to juice base, <u>not</u> letting it boil furiously, just for a few minutes to become well mixed, then turn into dish with or without spoon, cake at bottom, sopped in sherry wine & . . . jam, under these final conditions it would be called a <u>party</u> pudding!

Spike Milligan's
Spaghetti Dolce

Approx 8 oz (225g) spaghetti, cooked al dente,
   no salt (about 8 minutes)
5 oz (140g) carton double cream
Two tablespoons brandy
Caster sugar to taste

Cook spaghetti. Whilst this is cooking mix together cream, brandy and caster sugar. When
spaghetti is ready pour over the cream.

George Orwell's Plum Cake

'Tea', also commonly called 'high tea', is a large, comfortable, informal meal, designed for people who are tired from work and have nothing to eat for six or seven hours. It has to consist, therefore, of something that can be got ready quickly, and it is usual to place all the dishes on the table at once. High tea, if it is a good specimen of its kind, consists of one hot dish, bread and butter and jam, cakes, salad or watercress if they are in season, and – at normal times when such things are easily procurable – tinned fruit. Sometimes the main dish is cold ham, tinned salmon or shellfish, but usually it is something hot: it may be some kind of toasted cheese, such as the delicious Welsh rarebit, or fried bacon, or sausages, or kippers, or perhaps stewed beef or cottage pie. No tea would be considered a good one if it did not include at least one kind of cake. Cakes are one of the specialities of British – more particularly of Scottish – cooking, and, like puddings, they are too numerous to be listed exhaustively: one can merely indicate a few that are outstandingly good. The best, and the most characteristic of Britain, is the rich, heavy plum cake which is so impregnated with spices and chopped fruits as to be almost black in colour. In their fullest glory those cakes are studded all over with blanched almonds, and at Christmas time they are even richer by being covered with a layer of almond paste and then coated all over with icing sugar. There are, of course, many other varieties of plum cake – a 'plum' cake simply means one that has currants or sultanas in it – ranging down to quite plain and inexpensive ones. The richest plum cakes, which contain rum or brandy, improve with keeping, and it is usual to make them some weeks or months before it is intended to eat them.

Ingredients:
  ¾ lb butter
  ½ lb sugar
  4 eggs

¾ lb flour

¼ lb crystallised cherries

¼ lb raisins

¼ lb sultanas

¼ lb chopped almonds

¼ lb mixed candied peel

The grated rind of 1 lemon and 1 orange

½ teaspoonful of mixed spice

A pinch of salt

1 glass brandy

Method: Beat the butter and sugar to a cream; add each egg separately and beat until the mixture is stiff and uniform. Sift the flour with the mixed spice and the salt, stir well into the creamed mixture, add the raisins (stoned beforehand), the cherries cut in halves, and the sultanas, the candied peel cut into small pieces, the grated lemon and orange rind, add the brandy. Mix thoroughly, put into a round tin lined with greased paper, put into a hot oven for 10 to 15 minutes, then reduce the heat and bake slowly for 3 ½ hours.

Sylvia Plath's Tomato Soup Cake

This letter written by Sylvia Plath's mother, Aurelia Schober Plath – which was sent soon after she visited her daughter in England in the summer of 1961 – shares a recipe which would go on to become one of Sylvia Plath's favourites. Tomato Soup Cake would become a signature recipe; she baked it on the same day she composed her poem 'Death & Co', for instance, and many times throughout her life.

½ cup shortening

1 cup sugar

1 egg

1 can tomato soup (undiluted)

1 teaspoon soda

2 cups flour

1 ½ teaspoons cinnamon

½ teaspoon cloves

½ teaspoon allspice

½ teaspoon nutmeg

1 cup raisins

Cream shortening, add sugar, then well-beaten egg. Stir in tomato soup. Sift all the dry ingredients and add these gradually to the mixture. Flour the raisins lightly and beat into the mixture. Bake about 45 minutes at 350, in a well-greased and lightly floured pan. (I just shake a bit of flour through the sifter over the buttered pan, dusting it lightly.)

You used to like an orange icing on this – about 2 tablespoons of butter creamed, icing sugar and orange juice. To make it special, I used to place walnut halves or quarters on the icing so that, when cut in squares, each square would have a piece of nut in the centre. I also make a cream cheese (instead of butter) frosting with orange juice or flavouring.

Dodie Smith's
Proper Strawberry Shortcake

I can't cook. When I was poor I got my food at cheap restaurants. When I made money I got someone to cook for me. I only wish there had been frozen food when I was young, the kind you cook in plastic bags, without dirtying a saucepan. So, in the circumstances, here is a truly magnificent feat of cooking. I've never made it, of course, but I've certainly enjoyed it often. It is *real* American strawberry shortcake and nothing like the pale imitations most restaurants over there serve.

3 oz butter, 1 lb plain flour, 2 oz sugar, 4 teaspoons baking powder, pinch of salt, nutmeg, 2 egg yolks, ½ pint double cream, 1 lb strawberries, ¼ pint milk.

Pre-heat oven for 15 minutes at Regulo 7 (425 degrees). Sift all the dry ingredients together and work the butter into them until the mixture resembles fine breadcrumbs. Lightly beat the yolks, add to the mixture and begin to blend, adding milk up to just under ¼ pint until the mixture is thick and smooth. Pour into a buttered tin and bake for about 12 minutes – test with a skewer to check that the cake is cooked all the way through. Turn out to cool.

Wash the strawberries, save a few choice berries for decoration, crush the remainder and sweeten to taste, preferably with icing sugar. Cut the cake into two layers and sandwich with the strawberries. Cover with whipped cream and decorate.

Gertrude Stein's
Nameless Cookies

Sift together ¼ cup powdered sugar and 2 cups white flour. Cream 1 cup butter and add the flour mixture slowly, little by little; this procedure, stirring rather than beating as flour is added, should take about 20 minutes. At midway point, add 1 tablespoon curaçao and 1 teaspoon brandy. When mixture has been combined, roll the dough into small 'sausage' rolls about 2 inches long and ½ inch thick. Place on lightly oiled cookie sheet 1 inch apart in preheated 275° oven; bake 20 minutes. Remove gently with spatula, gently sifting powdered sugar over them while still hot. Kept in tightly closed container, cookies will last up to 3 weeks.

Walt Whitman's
Coffee Cake

Pour one cup of boiling hot, strong coffee on one cup of lard or pork fat; add one cup of molasses, one cup of brown sugar, three well-beaten eggs, one teaspoonful each of cloves, cinnamon, all-spice, one half-teaspoon nutmeg, one teaspoon-ful of soda dissolved in a little warm water, flour enough to make a stiff batter. Bake in a sheet-iron pan one hour and a half in a slow oven.

Daphne du Maurier's Cornish Sloe Gin

Gather sloes, when ripe, during the month of September here in Cornwall. Prick each sloe with a silver fork, and place them into a clean, empty wine bottle, filling the bottle only a quarter full with the sloes. Then add two ounces of lump sugar and two ounces of crushed candy sugar. Top up the bottle with Plymouth Gin until it is full. Cork and seal. Shake the bottle or bottles twice a day or more for three weeks. Then put away for six to twelve months, when it will be ready to drink.

Evelyn Waugh's
Mulled Claret

For six persons.

Take 6 bottles of red wine (it would be improper to use really fine Bordeaux, but the better the wine, the better the concoction). Any sound claret or burgundy will do. One cupful of water; 2 port glasses of brandy; 1 port glass of ginger wine; 1 orange stuffed with cloves; peel of 2 lemons; 3 sticks of cinnamon; 1 grated nutmeg.

Heat in covered cauldron. Do not allow to simmer. Serve hot and keep hot on the hob. Should be drunk at same temperature as tea.

To be drunk during and after luncheon in February or after dinner on a winter evening.

Eudora Welty's
Mint Julep

Have silver goblet thoroughly chilled. Take half lump sugar and dissolve in tablespoon water. Take single leaf mint and bruise it between fingers, dropping it into dissolved sugar. Strain after stirring. Fill the goblet with crushed ice, to capacity. Pour in all the bourbon whiskey the goblet will hold. Put a sprig of mint in the top of the goblet, for bouquet. Let goblet stand until FROSTED. Serve rapidly.

Acknowledgements

We would be delighted to hear about any other writers' recipes that could be included in our collection; please contact us at editorial@faber.co.uk.

We are grateful to the following for permission to reproduce copyright material:

'Salad cream' by Margery Allingham, published in *Celebrity Cooking For You: Dishes Chosen by the Famous,* Andre Deutsch, 1961. Reproduced by permission of Peters Fraser & Dunlop (www.petersfraserdunlop.com) on behalf of Worldwrites Holdings Limited.

'Fromage à la crème' by Kingsley Amis, published in *Celebrity Cooking: Dishes Chosen by the Famous*, Paul Hamlyn, 1967, copyright © Kingsley Amis, 1967. Reproduced by permission of The Wylie Agency (UK) Limited.

'Instant mince' by Beryl Bainbridge, published in *Writers' Favourite Recipes*, Corgi,

1978. Reproduced by permission of Johnson & Alcock Ltd.

'Cherry cake' by Enid Blyton, published in *As We Like It – Cookery Recipes by Famous People*, Arthur Barker Ltd, 1950. Reproduced by permission of Hachette through PLSClear.

'Baroque cake' by Brigid Brophy, published in *Meatless Cooking: Celebrity Style*, Grove, 1975, copyright © J. L. Barkas. Reproduced by permission of Curtis Brown Group Ltd, London, on behalf of The Literary Estate of Brigid Brophy.

'Cold banana pudding' by Truman Capote, published in *Ladies' Home Journal magazine,* November 1968. Reproduced by permission of the trustees of The Truman Capote Literary Trust.

'Potato soup' by Angela Carter, published in *Turning the Tables: Recipes and Reflections from Women*, ed Sue O'Sullivan, Sheba Feminist Press, 1987, copyright © Angela Carter. Reprinted by permission of Angela Carter's Estate c/o Rogers, Coleridge & White Ltd., 20 Powis Mews, London WII IJN.

'Hot bean salad' by Agatha Christie, published in *Celebrity Cooking For You: Dishes Chosen by the Famous*, Andre Deutsch, 1961. Reproduced by kind permission of Mathew Prichard and The Christie Archive Trust.

'Zucchini fritters' by Laurie Colwin, published in *Home Cooking*, Vintage, 1988, copyright © Laurie Colwin, 1988. Reproduced by permission of Writers House LLC acting as agent for the author.

'Mexican chicken' by Joan Didion, published in *The Great American Writers' Cookbook*, Yoknapatawpha Press, 1981. Reproduced by permission of Didion Dunne Literary Trust.

'Cornish sloe gin' by Daphne du Maurier, published in *Writers' Favourite Recipes*, Corgi, 1978, copyright © The Chichester Partnership, 1978. Reproduced by permission of Curtis Brown Ltd, London on behalf of The Chichester Partnership.

'Mrs Runcie's pudding' by T. S. Eliot, published in *Wishful Cooking* by Emily Mirrlees and Margaret Coker. Published by Faber and Faber Limited. Reproduced by permission of the publisher.

'Bread pudding' by Nora Ephron, published in *Heartburn*, Knopf, 1983, copyright © Nora

'Devils on horseback' by Elizabeth Jane Howard and Fay Maschler, published in *Howard and Maschler on Food*, Penguin, 1988. Reproduced by permission of the Estate of Elizabeth Jane Howard c/o Jonathan Clowes Ltd.

'Gnocchi di patate' by Aldous Huxley, first published in *As We Like It – Cookery Recipes by Famous People,* Arthur Barker, 1950, copyright © Aldous Huxley, 1950. Reproduced by permission of Georges Borchardt, Inc. on behalf of the Aldous and Laura Huxley Literary Trust. All rights reserved.

'Brownies, Wendy' by Christopher Isherwood, published in *Celebrity Cooking: Dishes Chosen by the Famous*, Paul Hamlyn, 1967, copyright © Christopher Isherwood Estate, 1967. Reproduced by permission of The Wylie Agency (UK) Limited.

'Green pea soup' by Jack Kerouac, published in *Literary Eats*, McFarland & Co, 2014, copyright © Jack Kerouac, 2014. Reproduced by permission of The Wylie Agency (UK) Limited.

'Crab nebula' by Ursula K. Le Guin, published in *Cooking Out of This World*, Wildside Press,

1992, copyright © 1973. Reproduced by permission of Ginger Clark Literary Agency.

'Anna Woodhouse's pie' by Rosamond Lehmann, published in *Writers' Favourite Recipes*, Corgi, 1978. Reproduced by permission of The Society of Authors as the Literary Representative of the Estate of Rosamond Lehmann.

'Chicken with lemon and orange' by Doris Lessing, published in *Celebrity Cooking: Dishes Chosen by the Famous*, Paul Hamlyn, 1967. Reproduced by permission of the Literary Estate of Doris Lessing, c/o Jonathan Clowes Ltd.

'Stuffed mushrooms' by Norman Mailer, published in *The Great American Writers' Cookbook*, Yoknapatawpha Press, 1981, copyright © Norman Mailer, 1981. Reproduced by permission of The Wylie Agency (UK) Limited.

'Barbecue lamb' by Olivia Manning, published in *Writers' Favourite Recipes*, Corgi, 1978. Reproduced by permission of David Higham Associates.

'Steak en casserole' by Ngaio Marsh, published in *Celebrity Cooking For You: Dishes Chosen by the Famous*, Andre Deutsch, 1961. Reproduced by permission of Aitken Alexander Associates Limited on behalf of the Estate of John Dacres Mannings.

'Spaghetti dolce' by Spike Milligan, published in *The Celebrity Vegetarian Cookbook*, Green Print, 1988. Reproduced by permission of Spike Milligan Productions.

'Eggs à la Nabocoque' by Vladimir Nabokov, published in *Literary Eats*, McFarland & Co, 2014, copyright © Vladimir Nabokov, 2014. Reproduced by permission of The Wylie Agency (UK) Limited.

'Plum cake' by George Orwell, https://www. orwellfoundation.com/. Reproduced by permission of A. M. Heath on behalf of the Estate of George Orwell.

'Tomato-soup spice cake' by Aurelia Plath, published in *The Letters of Sylvia Plath, Vol II: 1956–1963*, Faber, 2018. Reproduced by kind permission of the Estate.

'Marmalade' by Barbara Pym, published in *À La Pym: The Barbara Pym Cookbook*, Prospect Books, 1995. Reproduced by kind permission of the Estate of the author.

'Fricandeau à l'oseille' by Georges Simenon, published in *The Artists' and Writers' Cookbook*, Angel Island Publications, 1961, copyright © Georges Simenon, 1961. Reproduced by permission of The Wylie Agency (UK) Limited.

'Proper strawberry shortcake' by Dodie Smith, published in *Writers' Favourite Recipes*, Corgi, 1978. Reproduced by permission of Film Rights Limited in association with Laurence Fitch Limited.

'Pâté maison' by Stephen Spender, published in *Celebrity Cooking: Dishes Chosen by the Famous*, Paul Hamlyn, 1967, copyright © Stephen Spender. Reproduced by permission of Curtis Brown Group Ltd, London, on behalf of the Beneficiaries of the Estate of Stephen Spender.

'Nameless cookies' by Gertrude Stein, first published in *The Alice B. Toklas Cookbook*, 1954. Reproduced by permission of David Higham Associates.

'Filets de bœuf aux bananas' by Noel Streatfeild, published in *Writers' Favourite Recipes*, Corgi, 1978. Reproduced by permission of A. M. Heath on behalf of the Estate of Noel Streatfeild.

'Chintz turbot' by Sylvia Townsend Warner, published in *Writers' Favourite Recipes*, Corgi, 1978. Reproduced by kind permission of the Estate of the author.

'Mulled claret' by Evelyn Waugh, published in *As We Like It – Cookery Recipes by Famous People,* Arthur Barker, 1950, copyright © Evelyn Waugh, 1950. Reproduced by permission of The Wylie Agency (UK) Limited.

'Mint julep' by Eudora Welty from *Literary Eats,* McFarland & Co, 2014. Reproduced by permission of the Welty LLC and Russell & Volkening.

'Dutch onion crisps' by Rebecca West, published in *A Kitchen Goes to War – Famous People Contribute to a Ration-time Cookery Book*, John Miles, 1940. Reproduced by permission of Peters Fraser & Dunlop (www.petersfraserdunlop.com) on behalf of the Estate of Rebecca West.

'Grits' by Tennessee Williams, first published in *The Great American Writers' Cookbook,* Yoknapatawpha Press, 1981, copyright © Tennessee Williams, 1981. Reprinted by permission of Georges Borchardt, Inc., on behalf of the University of the South. All rights reserved.

List of Recipes

Starters

Mains

Drinks